Songs For Boys Called Wendell Gomez

By John Doyle

Copyright © 2018 by John Doyle
Layout: Pski's Porch

All rights reserved. No part of this book may be reproduced in any form by any electronic or mechanical means including photocopying, recording, or information storage and retrieval without permission in writing from the author.

ISBN-13: 978-0-9988476-9-6
ISBN-10: 0998847690
for more books, visit Pski's Porch:
www.pskisporch.com

Printed in U.S.A.

Go raibh maith agaibh

Mother, Father, uncles, aunts, cousins, my late sister
Ken "Mr. Hemlock" Folan, John Greene, Andrew "Break a Leg" Clarke, Eddie Connolly, Michelle Godard, Enda "Carmine" Carr, Jonathan Dickson, Heather Stewart, John Harold Olson, Neal Grosvenor, Amos Greig, the late Brother Brendan - a good man, David Kane, Alex Dempsey, Anthony Smith, Gerard James Hough, Dickie Weldon, Paul O'Mahoney, John Warwick Arden, Monica Baron, India Pale Ale, Eoghan McGrath, Sandra Curran for politely smiling when reading my crazy ass poems, Miranda Eilers, Judy Edmonds, Dave - for agreeing with me about that talentless hack; Louise, Richard, Dorota, Shivers, Lieutenant Deegan and the K.W.E.T.B. crew; Ivor McCormack, Paul Brady, Steven Storrie, Susan Pallesen Rapley, Deep House Music, Mod Culture, Andy Lawless, Saint John Coltrane, Danny Wilde and Lord Brett Sinclair, Ralph - a proper team-lead, all those open-mic night organisers for giving *The Palookaville Putz* a shot at the title, Bernadette O'Shea, Duane Vorhees, that woman who smiled at me on train on Tuesday, the cat who appreciates me feeding it, Pat O'Connor and George Clarkson for having faith in me in the 1980s when every other teacher left me high and dry, Burt, and God,

and you, thank you.

This book is dedicated to those no longer with us, and those who have yet to join us.

Annette - thank you for helping me see the sun and moon and stars again xxx

Some of these poems appeared in some incarnation or another in the following - *Blood, Sweat, and Ink, The Maynooth Newsletter, Degenerate Literature, A New Ulster, Yellow Mama, Clockwise Cat, Duane's Poetree*

My gratitude to the editors of the above publications and websites.

Contents

Hello 5
The Acts of the Saw 6
It's Van Morrison O'Clock 8
Uprooting the Remains of Small Trees 10
To a Woman Disappearing Around a Street Corner 11
An Ulster Expedition 12
I Remember Little of the 1970s, But... 14
Liam 16
"Fotografies, Senyor..." 17
A Changing of the Guard 20
Kilcoole, County Wicklow 21
Radio Days, 1986 22
There's the Rub 23
Song for Diarmuid 24
Yes, You Were an Obsession 26
The Sky Intends Murder 28
Monologues 29
Burt 30
Nacimiento Del Rio Cabra, Asturias 32
The Last Testament of Kurt Cobain 34
New Hampshire and Its Photostat Machines 35
Single Fantasy (If I Was in N.Y.C. When I Was Pushing Five) 36
Horses Rising Dust, Barcelona 37
Owls 40
On Listening to Mermaid by Brian Bennett and Alan Hawkshaw 43
Frost-Bite 45
Prague 46
English Summertime, Avon 48
On Reading Philip Larkin's Dublinesque 49
Castelsardo 51
Glenn Ford's Endless Sepia Cattle Drive 53
The Time We Set Fire to the Hayshed, 1987 54
Copernicus and The Curragh of Kildare 55
Gorm i nGlas 56
South Dublin City Bedsit, 1975 57
Wendell Gomez 58

Time-Lapses   59
The Humming Blue and White of Dusk   60
On Watching El Espiritu De La Colmena   62
Benfica's Lousy Record in European Finals Was a Metaphor For You and Me   63
Let's Piss in the River and Make it Deeper   64
Warning   66
November 29th   67
Departures   68
How Many Songs From 1973 Can Guns n' Roses Fuck Up In One Day?   69
Andropov, Ronnie, and Me   70
Sundays   71
I Was Sorry to Hear of Your Death, Nonetheless   72
Quid Pro Quo   73
Seán Óg Ó Ceallacháin   75
Trying to Sell Home Security to a Guy Called Bernard, Oldcastle County Meath, September 2016   76
Monaco   77
American Cinematography 1971   79
Winter Sundown   80
The First Time Ever I Saw Your Face I Knew There Would Be Thunder and Lightning   81
Amber/Brown   82
A Fallen Tree in Carton Estate, Maynooth, County Kildare   84
Photograph of Ashby, Massachusetts, January 1950   86
Song for Robert Budd Dwyer   87
Almost   88
Student in O'Neill's Bar (5/5/15)   90
Requiem For a Lost Year   92
Street Ballad   94
The Yellow School Buses of America   95
Dimecres, Foscor   97
As If   98
Clan   99
The Winners and the Loser of the Under-16 County Final, 1991   100
Is It Possible to Survive the War of Armageddon...?   101
Upstate, Late-October   102

A Boy on a Motorbike, Musiore India   105
Song for Buck or Zeke, Somewhere in California   106
*A Eurotrash Beach Voyeur Reads The First Epistle
of Paul to Timothy*   107
Anthony Braxton Sundays   108
Phil Lynott, 1974   110
Vernon Presley, August, 17th, 1977   111
A Man Gathers Stones on the Beach, Antibes, France   112
The Siren of San Francisco   114
When It Rains and No-One Else is Around   115
Thomas   116
There's a Killer Roaming the Streets of Camelot   117
Our European Days   120
Sligo Landscape, January   121
Maritime   122
The Scene Where the Weeds are Plucked in Lamb; 1985   124
Highway of the Resurrections   125
There Was a Woman Called Mrs. Mooney Who Used to Live a Few Doors Away   126
You Remind Me Of Sir Nigel Gresley's Mallard   127
Spain   128
Moon   130
The Farrier   131
McKenna's Bóthairín, Summer 1984   132
People Don't Just Stop Drinking   133
Italia, Ottobre   134
Tuone Udaina   135
Australian Postage Stamp 1972 - Overland Telegraph Line 136
Australian Postage Stamp, 1970 - Celebrating National Development   137
She Swore She Would Ride a Scooter Through the Basque Country One Day   138
Hangover   139
Albino Luciani   140
When The Sligo Liner Passes Through Maynooth Again   141
Seasons   142
Outposts   144
The Crucifixion of Jeffrey Hunter, 1969   145

An Cois Farraige, Gaoth Dobhair   146
Goddess   149
Evening   150
Side Street Buildings, Irish Seaside Towns   151
Raymond Carver's Little Black Book of Muses   152
Ploughed Field Near Confey Railway Station, County Kildare   154
An Afterthought (Laytown Beach,
County Meath) 156

"Some reassurance in your own depth..."

The Style Council

"Is annamh earracht gan fuacht..."

Old Irish Proverb

"Mysteries are irritated by facts..."

Norman Mailer

Copenhagen, December 2012

"Souls are fires whose ashes are the bodies"

Kahlil Gibran

Hello

Each one said it;
that middle-aged man
whose tone attested headmaster,
Garda sergeant, wannabe lord-mayor,
I said nothing back;
there was a homely pair of Yanks
enjoying Oireland for the first time since
the husband's illness passed,
ingratiating themselves
with every rippled sunbeam the universe could give;
I said hello, we smiled, and caught a criss-cross
of flight paths like a crucifix both warning and protecting an
opened clutch of sky;
And I watched them slowly weld hands in a brace of jangling sun.
A kid jumped from behind
accusing briers,
he was salty, tense,
either having beaten a 90 year old man to death,
or running from some guy he owed a double-score to, for a less
than normal sized batch of weed;
the paper in the morning will inform
me if I was right to say hello - or not.

The Acts of the Saw

Each plot
comes to pass,
you respond through burning cork

on wine-hue nose,
your every move perfumed -
of ancient ash, of weathered beech,

and your plywood drone
anthologies,
in wanton leer of stumps;

I would study your craftsmen,
their hands wide as Nile,
water's gleam

exchanged for song,
through coke-bottle's grasp,
the jagged rust like blood

the saw would shed;
each severed roll
solved winter's lifeless-chills,

thickened rumps amassed
like tribal heads,
faceless;

I salute your masters,
ancient,
their wildness abound -

men who tamed jungle,
men whose skin sizzled with lime,
and the men who tamed and gathered oak,

their faces tanned in galleries behind me;
My thumbprints turn scorched
in awe, sensing their steely curtain's bow

It's Van Morrison O'Clock
For Amos Greig

From jazz-breathing
Volkswagen vans
I see police inspectors dance
with their well-educated daughters,
Tupelo Honey
tinting glens-misted scotch,
a few cows chewing through tufts
of June's chilled and tempted navel.
These statues
come to life in hieroglyphs of spatial change -
like a brambling abject
to winter's slips of stone.
I could carve their figures
in voracious ore,
in sentries who
gaze on French chateaus,
icy, blue,
like the sudden dim of day -
as father, and daughter,
sip their drizzled dram -
and a dance re-awakens;
I cross and bless my key with baptised ignition -
there is wheat that sings the songs of harvest,
corn whispering to be cut,
I'll keep these migrations scored in psalm,
bramblings and strangers
cool as Armagh hands
who push in motion, the blue patchworked sky -
the light-kissed train-tracks
crooning Hewitt's transcending tones

Uprooting the Remains of Small Trees

A remembrance of birch tree
clasps Arcadia's lung;
we'll siphon these flecks of muck - from sheen of nails, hands
sludgy, squeak
of apple not beneath our will - we
watch blasts of day
cower below gawking fence;
its snapping branches
(experts in this decorum)
line-up on concrete,
mano et mano -
they resemble the dead of the Viet Cong,
remarked upon in magazines, 5,000 miles away, a coffee-stain
its mark of honour.
We could line them against the shed for shooting,
these muck-softened, yet bitter-skinned chapters
of grandparents who upped and re-rooted calendars
wheezing on the clock of soil,
awaiting an alignment of skin,
tugging the uncertainty of death
from their unknowing stem

To a Woman Disappearing Around a Street Corner

Two seconds you gave me,
not your face, your twilight or dawn-drizzled eyes,
just a taste of your sculptured shape,
your hair huddled in gutsy strands.

Now you're everyone, everywhere,
the artery before me
an envelope ripped-apart, and its
faces - scattered letters, words bluesy-blurred in dateless spates

An Ulster Expedition
(Driving Through Counties Armagh, Tyrone, and Donegal, August 2014)

(i)
A peer of orchards
tease Donegal's breath on their cool-griddled span,
our gears blistered
and prophets ripe,
beneath this scope of grinning sun.

(ii)
The blazing gallop
of streams
are drum-rolls
Armagh broncos
edge toward -

shuddering
at their reflected days,
their collage of mustang spirit, of faces flat as lightning, on
dangling dandelion eve;
Sion Mills withdraws a glower; huffing, stalling,
a lag in tandem through this trotted equine-squint.

(iii)

Through this gaping esker
we eavesdrop grumbling cross-county roads,
an immortal hush
through cider's blur,
evergreens feral

from hasty-briskets of heat.
The apple-red zion
sent these hooves
sparkling through a peep of evening fire -
Gweedore, one less hour from azure-shores; waves hushed -
as uncommon dialect of surf

I Remember Little of the 1970s, But...
(For Miranda Eilers)

The library's closing soon,
the caretaker's getting psyched-up for some ball-game he'll
hardly win,
and his vacuum cleaner's wheels sound like the twister
from the *Wizard of Oz*,

whistling and howling;
a mustache-whispered man
collects his CD,
Pretzel Logic;

and I get a jones for the blackness of night
that kind of shit evokes,
when night was a place for twisters, and globules of rain,
and boxing on tv, and fast-food you collected yourself,

and dads watching the *Rockford Files* -
and just like boxing, someone got beaten
and got on with life;
and the caretaker's finished hoovering

and I miss the sound of wheels
like a parting twister;
and part of me secretly hopes he's angry at me for walking
his prudish carpet -
even if he's in the wrong for cleaning up too soon;

I want an old-school showdown,
in sepia - like the *Wizard of Oz* begins and ends,
the backdrop an open city-scope

only *Pretzel Logic*

can define,
punches and kicks splintered everywhere -
and Jim Rockford watches a cheap Wednesday-night fight,
drinking beer with Noah Beery Jr -

and his eyes hum blacker
than this onyx lump of night, the one
I must go to, and
press my far too soft face toward

Liam

Down in the deep,
down, down, the language of the sunken -
the deadest corpse of all it translates -
not you - *her*;
the stars heaved in silence,
not you, not her, now me;
I'm marooned without a buoy, in her murkiest depths,
you silent - from the speechless mouths of stars; her, drunk again
in the company of less-drunk boys

"Fotografies, Senyor..."

My window cannot rest,
the thickened lurking glass
carries the litanies of crestfallen night;

it's how you would expect it,
were a typewriter and some caffeine involved -
word for word, note for note -

the dental moon peering,
severed by the electric fangs of light
and the soot-cloaked clouds

bawling from feline stars,
yeah, badass shit is going down;
I wait for Philip Marlowe

to light up, then grimace from a still-healing rib,
watch his face dribble in
sweaty beads of rain.

It was the face I shone, Torrevieja, October 2012,
her smile lay precisely cut,
by glass that stole starshine from a roadside skip,

discarded near wardrobes, lovers' bric-a-bric,
and the smell of scorched evening
as we shot cannonballs of pool.

The moon burned holes on felt
as we stopped to take photos on the highway home,
a little drunk, the stars seeing doubles of themselves,

a cop pulled in, tugged his pork-white gut from belt,
"Fotografies, senyor"
I said,

and like that the sky had swallowed his entire life whole...
Tonight, his limbs come falling
and her quartered smile

spits out his stellar teeth,
tonight, count the whiplash rain
and the snakes hissing on Valencian roads, Philip Marlowe
laid out cold.

A Changing of the Guard

Silver sixpences
primed for descent,

April's surrender to Summer's smirk,
one sleeper among its ranks;

Wednesday evening
I watched the drool of rain

bully a slender latch of land
acres short of Celbridge,

and its anger
tore its winds

from pages
those who claimed they knew God

knew what *Étaín* could preach too,
floral dresses of white-wine girls

clenched shoulder high
in a snarl of shock-eyed shapes,

the fire of Saturday's heels
tamed in puddles,

lurking around
the tatters of marquee

Kilcoole, County Wicklow

(1)
Seagulls brace
for landing,
breath dazed,
evening a twisting slow-motion
a kiss from misty tide
rips at seams -
these frenzied winds considered.

(2)
A thrust of land invokes
itself on wobbling sea,
the bright bloom of vegetations drift,
its severed slumber through fluff-sparked strand -
while at lung-less heights
a webbed dusk
is further and further unwrapped

Listening to Van Morrison's 'Celtic Swing'

Radio Days, 1986

I feast and drink from annals' ash -
softened lilt in bonfire's gaze - I watch greasy numbers burn,
from the grief of *Farney* headmaster's-stuffed-guts clock, ticking

towards the precipice of Monday morning -
Roy Willoughby's encore of *Terenure 9 Sunday's Well 6*,
Phillip Green's parchment - *Sligo Rovers 2 Finn Harps 4*

blesses preceding Sundays -
as parson fumbles beads
in hands cut from rope; we listen -

Three Rock Rovers,
Shelbourne,
Stella Maris,

Benedicat vos omnipotens
De, Pater, et Filius,
et Spíritus Sanctus;

Mother knows we went to mass -
our blessings - the return
of crunch on driveway gravel

There's the Rub

The future dead
surround me, chatting
of funerals
they must attend,
when I let my curtains touch
they're making love,
creating future dead

Song for Diarmuid

He was a martyr to something, someone -
and that he told me once - the stench of weed
understudied by the whiff that wandered
from his messianic feet -
it was a hiding to nothing for me;
oh I could have killed him yes, but where do 21st Century martyrs hide-out?
The pool halls, the wretch of bars on side-streets, where men swing cue-balls in socks,
as a warning, the taste of smoke alive, 9 years after bans took place,
and 40 year olds in Red Square Jeans sit beside me, (uninvited) -
they talk of the day Korn and Machine Head grinded their cobalt cunning into town,
my whole life like a
blunted-rusted axe, from Paul Weller's endless mirage
of northern women's washing lines.
Yes, if he wasn't martyred already,
I could swing the boot and grind the axe,
and that 4 days without washing smell
the prosecution could weave and knead around me
like an axe - about to fall;
He was seeking gainful employment, your honour, when that final boot went in...
with standard *Stairway to Heaven* and Bob Marley bedsit posters as red as sunset,
and the fire that kisses me, and promises he'll soon be gone; soon.
And those pizza-boys who dreaded weekend nights and the roaring freight trains
like frightened kittens clicking on late-night runs past his nest, will thank me for saving them,
a holy-sandal wearing martyr,
his Sunday morning gospels -
de-mystified at last

Yes, You Were an Obsession

Yes, you were an obsession,
if nothing else, I'll grant you that;
me a sea-skinned Spencer Tracy,
salt mapped like flesh-scorched herring, tingling crucified hands -
it was your secrets I hunted
as you tried on your fifteenth pair of *Nike* shoes,
I wandered through the shopping malls of Spain
looking for a perfect Iberian you,
a peep in the lives of
Consuelo, Pedro, Juan and *Marie,*
a car-park moon and forensic stats -
rattling in *Hipercor* plastic bags -
their love, desires, shame,
mapped in the fortified-way they held hands
and filled their 4 yearly payment family cars -
a scented glow,
a sweet taste of lunar love;
You'd scrunch your toes
as I returned full-blooded, eyes pricked with a fury of stars,
thinking of battered boats
and line-spliced palms,
a season for the shedding of blood -
beneath your Janus-faced low-hanging moon

The Sky Intends Murder

The sky intends murder, tonight;
an evening's teeth drip of blood,
the taste of iron teasing,
the knives of lightning spat through the stumble of skinless trees,
the flash of nude, flesh, whole body - split between paint-thirsted spires -
the puddles gasping for a kiss - of last night's milky moon

Monologues

A girl is talking and talking, and talking;
and that's okay -
monologues need not be saved for days of wine and roses,
of sharpened blades fumbling morphine-rust.
A girl is talking and talking, and talking,
she tells no-one in this nowhere place
a rubber duck floating on the miniature pond
is just like the one marooned in her bath,
and it's Saturday,
that day she'll soon grow to hate,
when everyone talks and talks, and talks,
minus inner-monologue, no-one's listening anymore,
except the ambient hiss of snakes
and the gurgle of gold-diggers' emptied pans,
losing something almost said,
what a girl who spoke to no-one, nowhere, could have said; didn't

Burt

The calcium music
of stiffened tail
squirms like serpent -

lodged on vertigo streets;
one sidewalk lets oceans bubble, but as shadows of Proust,
biting on clay-tinted nails,
the other gap is vast unsung desert,

his whole body
joined like tail-less adder -
searching for the song of bone, of sand,

even water;
Precise
benedictions

which flow as air
catch hair
from wizened whip, black as a yard's evidence of flickered
anthracite -

he watches hours gurgle
down cloudy drains,
his witching hour separates moonless streets; later

he'll
gnaw through
the stiffening folds of night.

I watch him sleeping;
I unlatch a cache of stars and moonshine
still caught in the tailspin of soot-dangled cloud

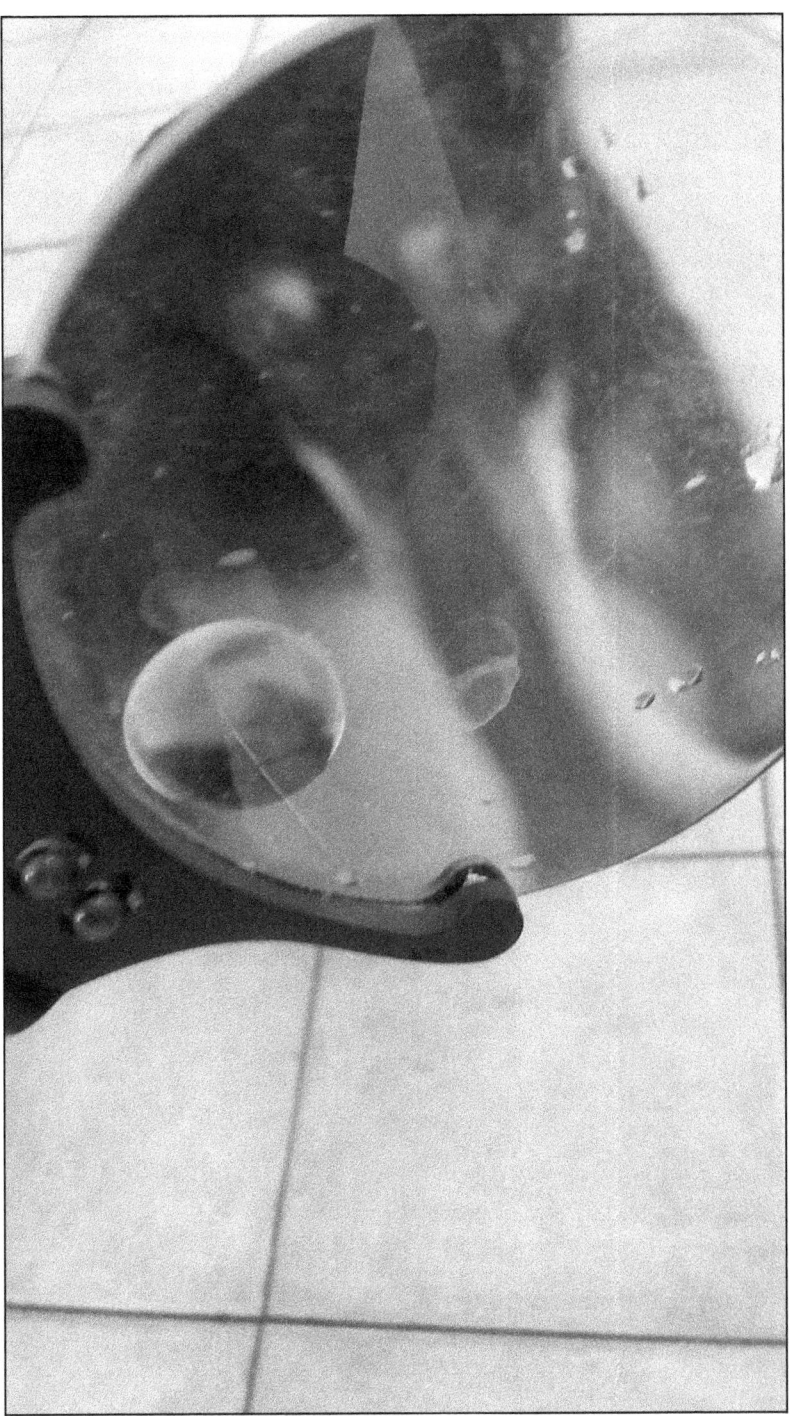

Nacimiento Del Rio Cabra, Asturias

A cottage soaks *Llanes*
in its devoted Latin stone,
a dawn looms in communions of light, through a glanced
yawning sun; we host daybreak's tender rites, as one - as the
same;

And the realness of
trees
from which hidden waters
appear

make real too
this gravid arch,
this sudden dreggy
ruffle -

on water
sifting muck,
on faces
virile

from green
blackened shadow
of drooping leaf, of parceled foot;
the realness

in Sunday quotes *Exodus* -
where water shows
its fears
for the first - and the only time -

its mother
and father
a pair of chattering shadows
whispered on frosted Latin stone;

And *La Borbolla* tears daybreak from its moorings -
the skipper's telescope
gurgling lens
on passing hooves in splattered mud,

the blueness
of Atlantic
almost
endless, the gelding's chassis surging from sea

The Last Testament of Kurt Cobain
If I'm going to sing like someone else, then I don't need to sing at all—Billie Holliday

Almost poetry,
isn't it?

how your garage roof prods somewhere
you're not too sure exists;

the silver spoon slithering deep in motion;
watch it Kurt, watch it biting back,

your lovesick and sorrow-fattened face,
a feedback hiss on cornflake-fix morning t.v. -

and for those 23 years it took me to say,
you were more than spit crawling down a camera, Kurt,

me frisky for the ass of Aerosmith
to yee-hah its leather carcass into town;

yeah, 23 years it took me, and what exactly do I say?
fuck it

New Hampshire and Its Photostat Machines
For John Warwick Arden

A crunch of leaves on Concord streets
are concertos of feet -
of recently-engaged, college secretaries;

they advance en-masse,
leaf-furrowed
epitaphs, disguised under hurried snow;

and on Tuesday
there'll be trial runs
for these brand-new photostat machines;

Is it Latin, maybe Greek?
this *photostat* machine - an Olympus or Colosseum
built on vestal-unmarried paper,

like feet touch indexed leaves - on streets
in Fall-time New Hampshire.
I think of secretaries

in horn-rimmed glasses, wobbling in heels
carrying boxes of A4 paper;
I lift a bruised and snow-smudged box

and help Rhonda place it in her station-wagon;
I think of Greco-Roman smiles indexed
on sheets of 1960s photostat paper

Single Fantasy (If I Was in N.Y.C. When I Was Pushing Five)

(1)
Uncles and aunts in hopscotch pants
emerge like sunflowers - from groaning staircased
apartments - (and I mean *apartments*, not "condos").

(2)
Outside are water hydrants where belly-buttoned girls dance the seven veils,
and other little boys' uncles play mouth organs with dogs who look upwards in their face -
like they're Saint Francis -

and all the animals gather round him on that parchment
in the church with the Irish priest called Fr. O'Malley, (I think);
who preaches on the block where aunts
carry groceries to their ballooning breasts in large paper bags
normally only seen

in cop shows late at night.
And girls who dance the seven veils politely stoop
to pick-up fallen apples and run after aunts carrying large paper bags.

(3)
In a cafe John and Yoko watch,
they talk about using this scene for the cover of the album
they will release as their follow-up to *Double Fantasy*

Horses Rising Dust, Barcelona

A corral awakens docile turf -
as sharp as day hides from moon,
as loud as drums descend from titian hills -

their floodlit chassis wrapping flame
on
wraithlike trees.

And the blaze of hooves
rise Epona from
drumlins of clay,

the shadows of
Roman sentry
revolved -

and day ripping its skin from salted-moon;
its conscripts
dragged - on scorching electronic hooves

Owls

Nocturnal of course, these dim-sung mantras,
these messengers stitched in the tangles of dusk;
their wings unwind in neon
streaked down raindrop-prickled streets,

and the purple vines melted, on stopwatch-smoldered shops.
You pause - in hope, for the fluttered fix of pairs,
your metropolitan frontier

crumpling past in Philip Marlowe macs,
kindled on the animation of night.
The owls set witching-hour in motion,
wailing babies chill their parents'

jangling spines,
and in every madrigal
their camera-lens eyes
could hoped to have known.

The mathematics is simple; on Spokane sidewalks,
Brussels boulevards -
I've seen how emphatic
the flickered shapes of breast on moons are

(especially in witching hour),
hauling tides from sleeping shores -
music that
powers sunlight for cities clung to its whispered map -

Helsinki, Algiers,
radio tuned to
a hiss of foggy Chopin,
Hilversum and Lisbon -

veins that glow
like metal cage,
that marry cobblestones to
mulberry nights -

and here they pause -
conscience of granite-stricken sky,
on people-shaped rooftops,
where you're numbed by the clicking heels of

laughter, outlined on the frames
of illicit reggae smoke, and shadows pours lives
like lightning-bolts'
electrified concrete cracks -

the urbane thunder
dismounted from *Riders on the Storm*,
cloud-flight on orb-skinned fresco,
dangling from placenta-splashed moon;

owls
witness anti-meridian's descent,
a pulling whistling wheeze, dead city shedding
skin, now on Labor Day

melancholy hitches a ride on these dripping lilac-hues,
inside their cast-iron guts, full tables, wine bottles
diapered in straw cantina fatigues,
and two nightbirds

glittered
in starshine - on the *Evening Herald*'s
nights-out page
in August 1982

On Listening to Mermaid by Brian Bennett and Alan Hawkshaw

Dusk; coolest blue,
buildings shine in cobalt glass,
and the lives of legs in windows cut from above the knee,

shaped - in a city's sketch of stars,
locomotives,
thickened black-hole smell,

and the secretaries' heels click their codes
on streets,
breathless in watching glass

Frost-Bite

The cold noise of dying day, glitters footpath;
motorways lying in wait epochs away; roaring, yawning

Prague

"The decision to return to any early scene in your life is dangerous but irresistible"
Paul Theroux *Ghost Train to the Eastern Star*

I was not city, country, nor town,
nor the Karlov Bridge where it seem everyone loves each other -
except men who spit their dreams on the glassy confessors of reflection,
as the swallowed river frightens itself to sleep;

I was not sunshine, nor nightfall,
bent like the swirl of pole-dancing trees
through the park
where I watch cops train horses - over the huddled loaf of wall,

and the waitress in the cafe
on *Pod Havrankou*,
was maybe the only woman
I've ever loved,

no, none of the above;
I've tried this beaten restless heart,
emptied of vanilla strands of a love-lorn dance,
watching each watching face

from a passing train that worms the superterraneans underground;
I sip lemonade, I watch *Law and Order*
from 1995
in *Marks and Spencers* cafe

subtitled in Czech,
as bridge wrestles mirage from sun,
as lovers stand at either side of bridge
as equine bolts

turns the city's wind chime light-bulbs blue -
and watching Briscoe drive away,
I see Logan holding fist
satisfied;

now I'm every city, every bridge of course,
every town
your kneecaps un-touch
and you like me loving you more,

things
together
from the knowing strands
of time,

like a waitress
with a loosened apron's clutch,
sips *Kozel*
beside us, on *Pod Havrankou*

English Summertime, Avon

Run through hip-high corn
in shawls,
in slow-motion;

the amber lights of Bristol
slip on curves of earth,
ovulating;

listening to Pink Floyd,
Grantchester Meadows,
sound ovulates on the blue amber curves of earth

On Reading Philip Larkin's *Dublinesque*

I suspect he took a Liverpool cattle-boat,
being ritually discreet,
then staying at a south-city Georgian house
owned by a middle-aged tight-ribbed lady
called Mrs O'Connell -
he everything Catholic,
she everything Protestant,
in glances that could hardly be considered sexual,
even moderately-repressed;
as he snaps braces on the weakness of sleeveless vest
his head pokes enclosed gardens,
washing-lines of tenements
dangle like his own sallow-curtained skin,
his naked oval
soothing out the exposed cracks where Dublin's
soggy nests ripple, in shockwaves
on the blast of an early morning Morris Minor horn;
Dublin, 1970 - his breakfast of pitied teacup
and chaste bitter-spooned saucer
soon solemnly sighed upon and forgotten,
hulking Georgian door followed shut
by "*don't forget to a bring a key, Mr. Larkin*"
"*Yes, Mrs. O'Connell*", another drizzle-lipped sigh seeking its
prescription.
He pokes that Sgt. Bilko head,
inky-rifled hunter, seeking specimens
of milk-floats
and shipping news,
the leather-hum of cricket balls
a puddle's jump away;
his hunt's nearly satisfied

as a funeral weeps its way down through the charred-bricked Macken Street,
he dreams its mourners
are subjects of Edward VII;
blood dripping like strawberry jam from his unleashed pen -
"Yes, a productive day, Mrs. O'Connell",
a Georgian-door smoothly leaving sundown's burial behind

Castelsardo

They warned us - *the rain rarely leaves,*
like tourists themselves -
a debauched platoon of football drunkards
lurking the unlit sides of midnight's cloak of streets;

Of course
Castelsardo forgets itself too -
these undervalued greys,
town of tangy sandy wind,

where thunder checks itself in,
and spends its silver flash of fingers
drifting down the mangled coast;
towns where the rickety chat of stone-faced men

softens cheese hung in cellars
for days of endless rain,
the satisfaction numbered in the folds
of clock-faced men's timeless arms,

and the scattered clinks of conversation,
in the rigours of calcium-clenched glass.
A vexed 1960s bus coughs its lungs
on the vertebrae of endless ascents;

so it must rain today;
though the rain rarely leaves, it rarely snarls or spits,
unless the Gods have been denied their conjugal rites,
the men whose bodies betray the narrative of bone

will somehow put that right,

Castelsardo's reddened drapes
softening in the hiss of benign rains,
and the harbour stone's chattered shivers, a citadel of foreign flames;

A sudden cough of grouchy clutch, a time of needless farewells

Glenn Ford's Endless Sepia Cattle Drive

I sat with her, silent
as Kilkenny kills its weekends,
Sunday to Friday - dusting windy concerto curtains
pushed outside, soon bedazzled;
she's Delphi's disowned bride, Melbourne, Stockholm -
wedged between this town I hear wants me dead too,
as Saturday dribbles down its drains,
and it wipes a napkin
across its fattened Don Ciccio chin;
and I lay with her, half-naked, a sort of pose, I suppose,
something forced, like couples who talk of future children,
man bearded, woman most likely called Chloe,
or the nearly-lovers that we were, who
tried painting starlight on walls last painted in 1972;
"I wish this was a wild west saloon", I tell her, "in Eugene, Oregon"
where my body last lay alive -
and I packed my corduroy pants,
setting off on Glenn Ford's endless sepia cattle drive;
I think she listened, I saw her fingertips move - away;
Thomastown swallowed by prairie stars,
Saturday heaved up from its trash-can lungs

Thomastown, County Kilkenny, October 4th, 2008

The Time We Set Fire to the Hayshed, 1987

Dessie, *Billy*, some kid called *Flynn*, and me;
And the spits of spark crunched closer and closer
to schoolboys' gormless giddy bone,

an hour of cackling hay
licking walls and welded-guilt,
on the cure of pre-teen stone.

Watch the harvest-fattened farmer tumble on the fold of fields,
nervous, heartbeats two to every penny, penny sweets no more,
boys on the promethean threshold - of men.

And the shame hosed from our sex-free souls,
sparks, stone, and that sun - oh, that sun,
coughing its fire from the pillowed-deaths of childhood's black;

Sparks, the guilt of shadows blackcurrant thick on facing walls.
And then that kid, the one called *Flynn*, Maguire and Patterson, his first -
his only *Page Three Girl*.

Never got married, Flynn, no wife, no kids,
an anthology of *Page Three Girls*,
and four years left of his sentence to run

Copernicus and The Curragh of Kildare
I.m. James Doyle 1921 - 1990

Clustered nights
found sky
mingle in clumps of
humid gorse,

the sheep
with graffitied manes
propelled -
in crinkling pens,

and you'd stroll from Athgarvan early,
your Copernicus
exiled in physics -
sealed in the orison of faith;

the bleated-hum of missing lamb
drew your rhythm
towards its fading light - soggy-foot firefly, kindling an orphaned cosmos;
your feet lay patched on gorse, a westerly blaze pressed through glowing
dancing digits

Gorm i nGlas

Aistrithe ag Miles Davis -
na dathanna ag titim, go dtí go mbíonn siad ceol gan dath,
fuaim gan ceol.

Tá rud éigin caillte san aistriúchán -
fuaim, dath, ceoil,
ag titim go deo, go dtí go mbíonn siad ceol, fuaim agus dath le chéile;

an ciorcal an anam
ag gluaiseacht
i ngach fuaimeanna, gorm agus glas i ngach anam

South Dublin City Bedsit, 1975

Heinrich Gerl's *Winged Ox*
guards bills that might
lie unpaid for weeks,

shoes should come off
when entering the low cut room,
an accord bursting with the best of Frank Lloyd Wright intentions;

The Dubliners and Le Brocquy
are poured from empty bottles
that rub shoulders like cactus-cluttered hawks,

gold-plated leaves
in smidgens of red,
an invitation to a fluttered-secret garden.

The Beanie cushions
cuddle a 30p weekly-rental Pye TV,
the smell isn't weed, they swear;

Paul and Ciara spent Wednesday
painting their archaic garden gate -
this gate stops Wicklow gobbling us up they think, giggling, touching...

Wendell Gomez

Nearly all her kids are on-board now;
she calls their names once more -
Selena Rogers, Danny Peck
and where's Wendell Gomez?
come on guys, anyone seen Wendell?

by the fountain
a duet of pigeons
flutter telescopic wings,
and they sound like Wendell
and his mom folding sheets on Sundays,

when pop is off in Helmand Province,
and the world's a lot wider in circumference than this,
and Wendell's teacher
still can't find him -
counting limitless equations two blocks, or maybe two
worlds away

Time-Lapses

For hours and hours the politicians' ping-pong ball clattered back and forth,
I didn't interrupt you - Please don't interrupt me.
By 9:22 it was absolute dark, t.v. set lay dead, smoke-signals their only transmission.
I'm sitting out-front
sipping beer,
I chew and slurp its metallic gob,
throw a few chips for the neighbour's dog,
grit my teeth.
I think of John Coltrane, my sister, my maternal and paternal aunts,
I'll stay, have two more beers

The Humming Blue and White of Dusk
(For Ennis Magill)

Twilight;
my awoken tongue
moistens in unsolved shapes -
like the jagged Kenyan bush

enunciates a dipping sky;
on summits near Kilcock
I watched Ennis latch his hay-shed gate,
a crack of gliding vowels

left his Antrim-mellowed throat,
syllables like smoke - pressed on death-less sun;
the radio hummed
in bumble-bees of fret-less bass

and *Bantu* chants,
moon breaking rank, skimming his hay-fattened shed -
this humming blue and white of dusk
the crimson-skin of drunken eve -

and *Evening Press* lozenge signs;
A half-shaved Bob Dylan
drove pick-ups through the
sighs of stiff-whippet grass, arched to its west from corn-fed breath;

April 1986,
occult cants and migrant sounds
like crimson skin when blood starts to clot;
Dylan's clean-shaven now, and showered,

the scrunch of gravel and his face a *Hinomaru*
of clotted tissue;
I share relics of confab with Ennis,
his throat cleared, mine a gargle of

mingled chat,
the fretless bass humming
like us - lost beneath Africa's skies.
The plovers and snipes

have drifted out of span slowly -
on Kildare's troposphere,
we'll carry its moon
from silver perch,

the sky and hermit stars
as tattered crosswords,
full of fives
and nines across - a duet of letters soon scribbled in

On Watching *El Espiritu De La Colmena*

Bones shatter as easy in death
as they tremble when flesh is cold,
all *personae non grata* now,
a sky's mouth a hole where babies appeared,
neither hungered, nor willingly born.

Sisters look for stars
behind the roof-shorn sheds of throat-less Spain,
the chuckle of beasts
the few words left fully-clothed;
if only they could grab those stars
they could fill holes in gaping marrow - in the loveless skin of monsters,
in flesh sparked
by flash of wire -
sparks that light those nights,
and let languages breath again, if only on a flashing broken-street screen.

The howling winds
garrote the bone, the poke of white gleaming from lies of muck,
in chattered skulls sparked with lucid eye;
Viva España
moans a single drifting sheet,
like moon swallowed in folds of endless black;
two girls like stone
absorbed by silence of wind;
Spain - naked now, the reel's flicker goes on and on

Benfica's Lousy Record in European Finals Was a Metaphor For You and Me

May 15th 2013;
and watch the three of us,
fucking everything up - yet again...

Let's Piss in the River and Make it Deeper

We've hunted clover mites
for weekend thrills,
the carnage grows notorious - on sanguine nestling hands.
Your descent downhill
gathers taut wild-grass braids,
screeches as sharp as shell-shocked debris -
beneath your toboggan's cascading thrust,
4-22pm -
not long 'til Coy and Vance
descend like under-ripened gods,
like clover-mite streaks
that trump the coal-black smudge
of *Speed Racer* tops -
with factory smoke clasping its claws
across the spire-pricked lungs of lords;
day gathering bags
for Cravens to Mullingar;
and the river's wheeze splutters
makeshift stone
we wobble our brittle gaits across -
you stop and think -
let's piss in the river, let's make it deeper -
I watch you reveling like ancient Rome's uncouth hordes,
chicken-leg like truncheon, clamped in one hand,
spilling wine across their faces -
with the other;
and I wonder how deep the river's gonna be,
when we're 9 years old,
when clover-mites learn the art of stealth,
when Bo and Luke suddenly find their way back home

Warning

Like rainbow shields on serpent's skin -
my purpose;
tutors' children pass -
watch their futures briefly mingle,
the face of broken windows,
knuckles mashed on pebbledash walls,
heads not right,
spreadsheet lessons at 42 years old;
the children read books in school today,
serpents with the strangest colours,
lethal in ice-cold skin, snapping fangs from burrowed soil;
I'm a serpent in a classroom window,
a photograph's shine in fluorescent light
warning children
how their futures may suddenly bite

November 29th

The day surrenders;
the chimneys' grip, undone;
scaffolds,
flightpaths,
cut the throat of rising moon;
I watch the death of blood-orange skies,
day undone

Departures

It happens,
that they're in and out of wards,
falling,
losing words
they bent down to scoop back up,
have heart attacks, then die;
bend over, pick up days,
forget them again,
love a little,
then turn around in bed some day,
go away

How Many Songs From 1973 Can Guns n' Roses Fuck Up In One Day?

The pub sound system
plays *Live and Let Die*, then
Knockin' On Heaven's Door;
and I think *how many more songs from 1973*
can Guns n' Roses fuck up
in one God-fearing working man's day?
the fizz gurgling from beer catching galaxies of departed dust

Andropov, Ronnie, and Me

I made the *Irish Times* front page,
December 1982,
some kid from somewhere else in some cosmos, beside me,
as men who drank *Rolling Rock* after we clocked off
in the factory - our John Deere hats
pronounced in rope-nested skulls.
The two of us danced all-sarcastic to Springsteen's
The River
'cos no girls would dance with the likes of us.
Historians will never know how it all went down,
he could be
interviewed on local Abu Dhabi T.V.
talking about how he
misses the *Guinness*, and doesn't intervene
when the presenter calls Irish "*Gaelic*",
not that a high flying Mick
would speak it anyway,
I mean come on, I was just turned 7, standing by a crib
in the *Pro-Cathedral*,
wet beds and Han Solo fantasies were all I had.
Sometimes I would show this page to girlfriends
in the Harry Palmer thrill of micro-film in libraries,
like nothing else ever happened, in my life,
Rolling Rock tinkled down staircases
from men wearing John Deere caps,
while Reagan and Andropov muttered about me
being a headline stealing little brat,
most of the time
it was just a set of keys from a librarian's jittery hands...
most of the time.

Sundays
Here is unfenced existence
--Philip Larkin

So this is the aftermath -
of weeks and weeks
piled-up;
they goose-step back to cities,
and teach their cubs to wave at trains;
oh Christ, it's a bloody aftermath,
of Mondays
wheezing on digital fog;

I think I'll spend this weekend
chattering with salty-stones,
maybe wave at kids -
who will one day teach their children, to wave back

I Was Sorry to Hear of Your Death, Nonetheless

Son-in-law?
prospects dug their graves in doubt
as princess and me cavorted like Richard and Liz,
she should have been at mass, that morning in Limerick,
I'm sure that's what you declared, her mother's pearls
so white, there's no way either of you could be equally pure;
So, I would not appear in those family snaps, even token faces
the not-as-friendly as he appears paparazzi
exiles, with behind the scenes consultations
in chemist shops in Wicklow - with 2 hour Christmas queues;
still, that night, a few days after Christmas,
we sank a few -
his coal-thickened old school stout,
my league of nations *Weissbräu,*
and we talked -
the women's soft-slippered feet
in miracles of silence
as the hall door clicked shut,
moonshine a surrogate lens
at last;
this photograph I remember, you and me, so real,
jowls of doubt less-pronounced, on your lunar-softened face;
click...

Quid Pro Quo

Inlets query meanings -
most days;
green, green breath of sky,
the hill-side burnt ochre,

and the sea
obedient to its glass-hollowed moon -
while gulls shake off our limpid pace, briskly amused by nets of herring.
Dipping below

the mystic grass
wheat tickles our tempered skin -
It weaves our lives in magic and wildness -
and leaves our grumbling bellies hungered;

the howl of ore and pungent diesel clocks a passing Navan train,
and water mellows chalk-whitened heels,
loose dogs rustling past -
and we wonder, briefly,

how deeply this sun wounds our seeping sky,
how light burns its circle
like the hand of August's craftsman, of sanded tightened arc -
yet nothing gives up its ghost, no, nothing ever;

we touch water's edge, wash clean our lives left pressed on grass,
our pants turned-up
leaving pools to flood this coal-fire pier,
not quite lovers yet - no; but something burns, something breathes,

we'll find it

lurking in each other,
like the glass
promenades look-up to seek their moon,

like our footprints dragged on sand
watch oceans
fumble, then leave our pressings whole -
unfettered

Bettystown, County Meath

Seán Óg Ó Ceallacháin

To live by a large river is to be kept in the heart of things
John Haines

(1)
Lixnaw, Clogherinkoe, Eastern Harps -

a shake of muck-caked boot silhouettes fluorescent glare;

antlers brushing themselves clean of battle, sharp-suits
ironed for long-wave's evening call.

(2)
Man-O-War, Shelmaliers, Ramor United -

winds pulsate in Sunday tenor tones, mud-squish field,
scything westerly rain,

and boys harnessed on Atlas' shoulder - their faces willingly
marooned on squelching turf.

(3)
Brick Rangers, Mount Sion, Postal Celtic -

a final whistle's silver bullet punctures callous throbbing
cold.

The metaphysical seer chips names on Sunday-glinted stone,
a typewriter's font set in *Ogham*

Trying to Sell Home Security to a Guy Called Bernard, Oldcastle County Meath, September 2016

"I won't be buyin' any off ya today"
Bernard's leaned on gate - leaned, fattened - fixed on that field the
young buck from some foreign parish owns;
A fertilizer-bag cloaks his gammy legged-shame.
I undress my pitch, alone, ashamed, in spits of rain -
"think of the benefit, Bernard"
*"long hard winter, it's more than city boys you need
to watch for, you could fall on that leg of yours"*
his stare dangles from that stalactite-poke of railway bridge
two minutes walk away, stripped of smokey-bone
and an engine's roar that un-whitened skirts,
its rails sold in Nigeria, 1963.
Bernard mumbles on about his sister - in Ballyjamesduff,
she's 3 sons now,
one wasting time in college, I think he muttered Cork,
"It's okay Bernard, I've to be back in town soon, nice to have met you"
his talk's unabated, unravelled in spools of wool on fences in fields
outsiders own, was it Ballyjamesduff? Was that where his sister lives,
with 3 sons, and one wasting time in college - in Cork...?
Blackness falls; that sudden.
I'll hand them back this badge, make it Monday,
I think how deep my heel cuts soil with shovel,
soil with life to give,
with the rattle of wheels on steel under fertile bridges, two minutes
walk away;
that sudden; no blackness falling

Monaco

Her face reflects
George VI, Onassis, 1950s mob-built hotels,
her maiden smile uttered

in waves of cellar-whitened wine,
John and me resist the urge to swear;
and her colours gleam through heralds,

a coat of arms tanned on rocks
near Eze; she speaks of horses
groomed in youth,

Bertie Windsor's
smile unfurled as flags at death of dusk.
"Monaco", she tells us

"was nothing 'til the mobsters came,
the palace was full of weeds
and Grace Kelly was some Irish girl's name"

Monaco; as we stand,
ocean blue
charters carousel-tanned veins -

she listens through
chimes of glasses almost-full;
we rummage through our lives, what stories could we *possibly* tell?

American Cinematography 1971
(For John Harold Olson)

Deserts were the first thing we tamed,
tarmac whipped
on serpents' nihilist backs,

then came the Clydesdale -
branded, shadows forged in dust;
we swore we saw genies

as hooves cooled
in steam from bubbling troughs,
and then there was us,

heads specs of light,
that crossed a map
of sun-filled camera glares;

in 1971
our kindled bones
are all the rage,

circles and circles
of sun
bind our bodies, on closing reels,

Bacharach, Pete Duel,
Burbank California,
genies arisen, from sizzling desert tar

Winter Sundown

Sunday's embers soften
west -
easing wind,
a few leaves murmur -
in suspicion, then at ease,
day swiveling to its slump;
westerly the crackling in
tea-leaf chatter, suggestions
of turfy fire,
the west taking hold of torch -
for now

The First Time Ever I Saw Your Face I Knew There Would Be Thunder and Lightning

Alghero's hands dangled
on your clock,
where moon was sunken, moored
for hours -
and the brown hues of dust
where Sicilian cattle scorched and tanned muffled soil,
washed purple-black skies
to a day of orange
a man saw shimmer on his daughter - in her second-hand
wedding dress;
6 a.m - dawn called native birds to gargle salt
and lemon song;
men wore the same pants every day,
their faces knitted like cracks on maps
the hour-hand hid in yesteryear's 7 A.Ms;
Santa Teresa's mostly at peace now -
the bony-arsed blessed virgin
out for the count; my day slides in through cracks in lime-scald
stable walls,
I watch Sunday spark this monster closer to life,
I brace myself for storms she'll bring, the whine of purple-black,
and the guts of 8am - the day already meandered - and here it is;
the belch of Gods
in a rage of gut; the pyrotechnics soon will follow

June 2008

Amber/Brown

1.
Anglesea Road; September
slipped itself from my clasp,
embalmed leaves
marking my scattered lumpen steps.

I watch Vivaldi's gusts in
burned-out sparks,
the fire of Xarpo poised,
mummified round trees -

October; sea-winds duel
with archaic street-lamp stands, middle-aged Killiney swings
in corduroy and tartan skirts - I turn, peeking for
the crunch of uptempo heels.

2.
My house hums in brown
tonight,
the sun conducts its encore; now our bodies shimmering in dusk;

the median state
of day and night
stands as a nation of its own -

my house as fortress,
a copper flag
catching this as of yet, undecided breeze;

3.
I watch April's curtain drape all around me - I, the bronze

sun-freezed monarch;
I pass coins among scrimmaging birds, rooks like fossils on
these terracotta stones

A Fallen Tree in Carton Estate, Maynooth, County Kildare

Salt-crisp fingers
cosset tempered bark,
a glissandi of snails
itching in metronomes of day;

Oriental spice
and wardrobe
redolence
narrate

children,
who listen nearby -
like chattering birds, another language
will soon ascend;

April plants every seed, light
unzipped in caramel pockets of soil,
the fallen,
the rising,

those content to stand
and be immersed,
the sunken footprints
and sighs - on medium-rare tints of earth -
fire,
water,
unseasoned
giggle of life; brewing a stormless wind

Photograph of Ashby, Massachusetts, January 1950

In Massachusetts it's winter -
a gull's
snow-shook wings

cuckold in
cell-bars made from glass,
and the gull's see-through wings

fly solo -
from Ashby, Massachusetts,
its lineage

of babbling witches
who cackle snow from swollen roofs.
The mislaid-years drown in the beige withdrawals of slush,

in a calender's
unexpected
thaw; Harding, Coolidge - footprints carved from dustbowl mud;

and the photograph
of Ashby, Massachusetts
is wingless, its metronome pale; exactly frozen

Song for Robert Budd Dwyer

City marks its talons - day by day, your swollen frown a glare of ice -
in the glass of frigid face; it pushes, then retracts snow-grey mounds,
the days of sighs and jowls,
the light from snarling camera - that triggered sparks
from your unstinting fire.

Pushed further, further back,
your hind-legs lock, your claws tingle like the starving jaws of knife;
the city
that swallows you, its mouth an abstract of havoc -

like roots from angry trees
squeeze rust from coppice-vanished trains.
Your wife's at home, t.v switched-off;
she thinks of early supper,
how the grandkids will drive you nuts
in the year 2009,
the edge of town trains split through their core
by the hind-leg of marauding trees - their leaves a leviathan of sudden fire-red blood

Almost

"Still I Dream of It..."
Brian Wilson

"Under neon loneliness/motorcycle emptiness..."
Patrick Jones/Manic Street Preachers

A ghost paints herself whiter than
snow that almost fell around us, between us, perhaps;
her bones burning through leather, through the clasp of air
that washes evenings from the endless dead of highways,
of Helvetica signposts where towns end in names
that tell me nothing,
that gave me life, almost;
and the dash of rum trembles on tables near floors where we watched
Voodoo tamed and its warrior demystify its dance,
but I dreamed that somehow it could enamour us,
in orange glasses shone on whitened face,
the kiss of leather and silent broken heart,
and the sunset laid out in stripes like dead hells' angels
on highways where Helvetica spells her name
in a flash of 2:22am - and the lights that blind her kiss
in flickered fits on face-starved pillows,
blood slowly pink
in snow,
like the colours we once touched,
hand painting skin,
the rattlesnake cough of pining child, and flashed fingers of withdrawal,
and a memory killing what was almost ours,
leather and bloodied nose
and the infant fires behind her
driving pistons into a saddened curse of shattered night -

orange,
red,
black leather -
none of these claimed by the scorch of sunrise, nor the whimpered farewells of
setting sun -
in body bags stamped with Helvetica seal;
I watch the highway, from a distance measurable
only in years -
almost, if even that

Student in O'Neill's Bar
(5/5/15)

She's what Eric Satie
pours in his melody...

Requiem For a Lost Year

Years falling flat-footed from the clock-pillaged face of earth -
of this, there's little we can do,
for those lost, irretrievable, sentimental items left behind on trains;
You smiled once, your coffee's steam jiving like numbers in love
with grandfather clocks, you laughed and mentioned
lost-property desks for orphaned years -
for the times you lay screaming,
your fingers' clutch lost from buttercup fields, your
brothers, sisters, screaming all round you, your face
patched on shattered clock, summer, 1982; your coffee ice-cold in
its suddenness,
for years that rolled like lemmings over cliff's blood-ripped edges,
huge waves of limbless numbers, crashed off rocks, dismembered
drowning years,
your lost-property desk left unmanned - trains lifeless
in the sidings of centuries.
Do you remember that year you woke-up sweating?
knowing
summer was already gone?
Your kin knitted in beside you;
oh, what little they could do...
I remember well, my hands pressed on winter's glass next door -
the sun sank so fast it set every tree in the west ablaze,
my face bloodshot in glowing mirrors, my eyes filled with numbers
that could never last.

I don't recall which beast the Chinese named that year for...

Street Ballad

Clouds float in the same pattern only once
Wayne Shorter

New York City -
raincoats flap like
stars and stripes,
whispering pool-hall doors -
in coastal winds;
Men called Benny wearing black berets
watch Cadillacs sizzle on light-splattered streets,
the streets smaller than emptied fists,
and un-heeled skirt-suit women attach sneakers
reclining from cabs;
The street remains small, bars aligned like shattered bone, and peace
is wrapped in patterns of silence,
the silhouette freedoms of night;
Neon drapes Fr. Rossi's confession box -
the Hudson's ships howling from emptied stomachs
where the waters gush, and lights tell me
someone, somewhere,
hums this same song;
the street's listening, I feel it breathing, hissing...
Everything speaks like fire
when orange rains implode,
everything turns to red, and the music grabs my eyes...

The Yellow School Buses of America
To interpret is to impoverish, to deplete the world...
Susan Sontag

The breasts of earth
pinch morning's light from sun,
I watch them
watching me -

leopard-skinned, bald as car-less tyres,
their pores plugged with
deathless telegraph-wire;
the milk of words is soft, smoothened,

a goose-bumped sun
coughing
medleys of dust,
watching too -

aware felines may strike;
In Daly City I see the
school-buses pass,
yellow as Warner Brothers' sacred reels.

A woman pokes a vexed hiss of rattlers,
walking-stick like Zorro's blade;
creatures
recoil -

like David Mann,
pebbles calmly thrown at highway's carcass;
If God is myth, then so too am I,
yellowed dust, the hum of words

leopard-skinned,
endless;
The school bus leaves, I dream the driver's Marcella Platt,
I count the languages and lives in its belly

Dimecres, Foscor

My garden never smelled like *Camarles* -
now these rains pinch
silver knuckles through its soil...

As If

As if born
from twisted-scraggy branch,
the bird-song echoes trees
trembling in lumbered wind -
the stolen breath of starry chill
a sudden dip,
in starlight's chasms;

I watched starlings
hunt, after the spats-clad mob of rooks had left,
like useless paparazzi
tailing a soap star crawling home -
as if born from twisted scraps of ink,
the soap star's dress
like crumbs
starlings came and nibbled,
as if born from some useless rotten need.

Their headlines are crumbs
between the cracks - that spit fork-lighting through the gums of garden paths,
the letters they pluck at, little
worms laughing,
unafraid;
as if re-born
a morbid headline act; a life not yet written

Clan

Shrill caws tell me rooks are
done, shredding through the failing of days,
their evening dragged in the clink of bottle, in sinking sapphire
streaks;
my uncles' gaits hissed through mumbling wheat,
Autumn's
hopes of Godliness

giving cadence to their scattered seed;
and now the rains confess, and sponsor willing rooks,
who furrow my family skies into claws of tattered reds.

A teasing hiss
pelts gravel-chomped graves -
their shadows an effigy,

like Sopdet blowing seeds on
handpicked fields,
Illumination;

I stand with cottages, standing in turn - *Joe Murphy, the McGoverns* -
benign rust voiced on
the rattle of Dunboyne Road gates, their evenings
bluer than the skin of moons,

and their faces rustling between the peer of stars;
the last man emerged from the final train to Dunboyne;
he stands here, watches trains arrive once more

The Winners and the Loser of the Under-16 County Final, 1991

May 15th looms, my schoolyard stench of vengeance -
I ransack the unguarded litter, where cenobite sacks
are comatose curates -
unable to fight
a boots and fists de-frocking.

It's my first kill,
my first loop on the chains of man,
the boys honking past on the Moyglare Road
wave their brasso-slithered trophy,
my name hardly whispered;

their Alamo's unfolded on chilly tongue-sharpened grass,
cut in fractured knuckle, their clinks of
pound-shop medals,
draped in the grief
of lowered-noon;

I saddle back to camp, dust
choosing its graves, faces in passing windows
returned
to clock-softened seats,
litter scattered like Alamo corpses - everywhere, nowhere;
like pound-shop medals...

Is It Possible to Survive the War of Armageddon...?

Watching the stupid fuck right now,
and hell, I'm not so sure,
if he could even hold that pool cue straight,
I'm not sure he could see far enough to take the infidel's eyeball out;
he says it's been 3 years since he last drank, apparently he found his religion behind bars,
that's the rumour doing the pool-hall toilet gossip rounds, but still I'm not so sure,
like last week and the week before
when he threw shapes like his shadow was Sonny Liston,
like he was something special in 1964.
An evangelist hands out a step by step guide - outside,
but he's too busy speaking in tongues
to even realise -
this man with the broken nose on the ground below him
was the one guy on his side.
Yeah, I guess not.

Upstate, Late-October

Gangling ferns arch inward from men
shielding shopfronts - waiting for life to take a little bait,
any bait;

October's pointless now its clocks have changed - its nimbostratus
belly gouged messianic-red, their reefer smoke framing the yellow-
yawns of moon.
Our shivering car's fraught with the stinking

ugliness
of Tuesdays,
it's a war-hardened witness

with two unmarked roads
ahead -
we see nothing of course, nothing but the choked-language signpost,

its boast
of bullet holes -
if it were deeper in forbidden land,

like Wyoming before it was part of the U.S.A.,
and knew its name looked exotic
in 19th century font

in a lingering Don Siegel reel;
bullet holes in towns
where old people stand on ladders under lung-black covers,

taking photos of city-folk who pass -
men called *Henry*, their wives' heads watered with Eunice.

We see nothing of old-men's bodies,

knuckles warned in ink, driven by Sam Colt's coital twitch -
we'll let death (or the looms of dying) fill these barstool
holes,
its colours

stay on red, little else -
something always gives, that's the constant;
death, resurrection,

a road naked and nameless to its
rat-gnawed grit,
to a homicide soon called *night*

A Boy on a Motorbike, Musiore India
(For Paul, Rose, Jane, Siobhan, Louise, Nick, Jitu, Fergal, Amanda, Ethna, Lauren, Fergal, Robert, Timmy)

The baked bone-dry earth
gapes cracks for Ry Cooder's chords,

India - monsoon season leers -
early-warnings tapped in rust on a passing flesh-crushed
train;

near Musiore our mini-bus
absorbs bikes

wobbling under threes, fours,
packed with lives

staring back
from bitter dusty

T.V. screens,
t-shirts baptised

in pre-monsoon shrift;
one kid's stare lingers, that crackling eidolic stare,

he swipes his breath from sallow seconds - then,
like a shattered clock he's gone -

like a snake stitching water-gurgled cracks, minutes and
years bubbling in the hole

Song for Buck or Zeke, Somewhere in California
(For Steven Storrie)

There's always a blue-collar type in the *A-Team,*
sat on a pick-up truck, baseball hat, sleeveless jacket,
Neil Young shirt dribbled with tobacco-chewed growl -
It's easy cash, isn't it? because the local mill shut down -
and guess what - you'll cause a shitstorm tonight at the local-hall
for wrong-skinned kids - run by some young naive Guatemalan padre.
Applying a mix of Marxist theory and Bukowski aesthetics
I would advise this week's model, *Buck, Zeke,* or whatever his
poor despairing church-going parents called him, to rise-up against his
Charles Napier/Bill McKinney/Dennis Fimple-cast boss,
rise-up brother, join the masses down at the local pool hall/bar
where you can sip beer from bottles, watch the ball-game live
from exotic L.A.,
and harmlessly pat the asses of 19 year old bar-girls in Daisy Duke
shorts and white patent pumps;
just think, before you climb on that pick-up truck,
because, like Miss Carmichael back in first-grade
when she wrote you off,
I truly believe the odds are against you; just like B.A. Baracus
and the cornflake box full of milk 4am insomniacs do now right now -
you poor misguided fuck. And it will be such a shame really -
as that adult-education and empowerment course had been going
so well for you.

A Eurotrash Beach Voyeur Reads The First Epistle of Paul to Timothy

Solitude produces originality, bold & astonishing beauty, poetry. But solitude also produces perverseness, the dispropor-tionate, the absurd, and the forbidden
Thomas Mann, Death in Venice

I'm a melodramatist,
a man who seeks sin
to mould a trope his lesser self
can fit, like a sinner's glove fits glass-cases
in a somber hill-clenched church
overlooking some Riviera town,
and it's March;
and the sinners have yet to come.
And I put my lens away,
my ponytail the upper-half
of my arising cross,
my feet cool, gentle,
in holy water seas;
It is then I must breathe, then I set myself free

Anthony Braxton Sundays

We dream of Anthony Braxton Sundays,
our hands erect in prayer,
that constructs itself from water, from whirligigs of fire,
we drug ourselves in neon,
in highways
and the cool edges of city-stiffened
brick;
she's beside me now, a lamp
yellowed in moonshine, in the fuzz of unravelled dusk.
His music haunts,
divides, and makes tattered-hostages of us,
as if we were nothing,
no, nothing but shapes
blocking yellowed-moon,
and the red, red corners of cities,
that open their teeth
and bite
another reel - from these blessed Sundays

Phil Lynott, 1974
(For Gerard James Hough)

I wait around in 1974
and sit on buses stagnant, yet beautiful in *Merrion Square*;
I sit on black and orange *Craven* trains

singing *Showdown*
through the lens of
gold-rush zippers, where night bruised its skies on the rolling sag of sun

Vernon Presley, August, 17th, 1977

The longest night only seeps so far,
and if infinity expands - then it too has limits,

and you see that fetal pose, clenched in bijous of stars,
and you watched your boy, pants pulled down,

and thought it would be him, hollering your parting croon;
something in the stars missed their cue, Vernon.

But infinity spins in circles -
around and around splicing stalks in fields of black,

and as your boy's girl's cubs
dance as Tupelo comets,

a bijou of stars
sparkle - in mellowed tufts of black

A Man Gathers Stones on the Beach, Antibes, France

Present waters
chokehold words,
his rejection stuttered, in the brash concerto of rasping wave;
huddling these limits
he could cast odium on Algiers, a message in shattered bottle
scattered gulls descend and clasp -
uneasy, beaks clenched and numb -
in sickness and in health
'til death us do part -
the sea's his christening,
his feet and hands - soon his lips, seek to bless.

By five-past five he, she, stride this font of surf -
chilly stones they trade as shimmered gold, unneeded words

12th January 2017

The Siren of San Francisco

Twisting like a tree-trunk
with merely summer-time to lose,
the leaves drive onward from their tribe - on the freckled
patch of bay,
on the turquoise-gaze of teacup houses,
San Francisco, cold Spring morning;
Southwards the clip of breeze soften steps,
her face an escape of morning moon,
the sun creeping up behind her, the sun as red as her sudden
unbottled smile,
the flump of loafers, calm - on the depths of triggered-hill

When It Rains and No-One Else is Around

I mimic that previous moon,
whose drowning
was little more than murk-filled puddles
and longwave radio crawling up walls -
in wheezing lines of French;
I remember mornings after,
of exploding skulls and breath that seized
nations by their gut,
the clock stout and cherry-faced on my sterling wall;
there are lovers who never die,
they merely grow fat, and sit and wait
for rains to fall; they recall
what little they held,
in their atlas-palmed grooves,
between pattering voice,
between an ocean of scowls -
and still the moon knew us all, its lungs ready to burst; its spears
rattling my mirror-ball again...

Thomas

To a future cleric, Maynooth College, a few years ago

A face they say
speaks its words
before the mouth awakens,
a softened glen betrayed in crooked smile,
a less-brighter brother's ecclesiastical credentials -
let slip - in those side-street dustbin brawler's eyes.
Remember Thomas, my back turned
and your motions, though biblical yes,
more aligned to Judas, or men blocking light from Christ's
pre-resurrection shadow,
the sneer that cut the breath from lungs across Samaria;
Those acres daddy ploughs every day, Thomas,
whether it needs be, or not,
stand as idle land, idle minds, chaff that nurtures idle souls,
the trope blessed with enough lies
to fill the glens for a thousand more.
And if I lie in the hail of thunderstorms and crashing rocks
will you give me a final rite, Thomas,
your crooked crosier straightened -
on your soft-pink sneer-stuttered face?

There's a Killer Roaming the Streets of Camelot
For K.B.

"the Interloper was a baboon baring his canines,
screaming and strutting to scare off a predator"
Joseph Finder *Company Man*

4:22pm - you've clocked off early -
then silence -
calmly clamped to the ribs of unrelenting cities.

This is as unrequited-death should be -
that it's largely silent, bloodless, followed
by beers paid for by the man; in the case of killer - and victim -

your appearances saving face, nothing more.
Gacy and Dahmer, *now they were different*, you think,
snapping pencil like typhoon executes twig,
their bosses, demonic figures cut from within,

silent,
invisible;
This one's silent too -

and in nightmares spiders suck numbers from gaunt
bone-sunk clocks
over tap-drip kitchen sinks, you - helpless sucking breast
on rope-bridge November nights;

I saw him once,
slamming doors on horizons that shattered glass
in boardrooms in Chicago,

his exhaust pipe
of crushed bone
and muttered word,

of glass that kisses glass
then spits back
in buildings that face other buildings at 4:22pm.

And I watch you walk away,
you're roaring drunk and the city
jumping and screaming like helpless widows all around you,

and it flashes in sickened blurs like you've been poisoned,
and the laughter of traffic lights
and poking fingernails of rain are all you have, your whole
career straddled on the periphery of these murk-filled ranks.
As I made it home, I heard a newsflash,

I clamped my curtains shut so the city couldn't press its
fingers through me,
if you see this man do not approach, the news anchor said,
and my two buttons at the same time dialing fingers

wrenched out another microwave T.V. dinner,
I've got to face this fat-fuck Monday morning,
and he hasn't introduced his wife to me yet;

A drone of murder screamed
from an elevator's sanguine torso,
the shriek of Tuesdays as it reached bottom floor,
it kindled my shivered bone as manservant

to this well-rounded king of banal,
the most silent and succulent of killers,

roaming the streets of Camelot.
I'm next I thought;
I cross-examined the lift's evangelical glass,
saw the city grit its night-time fangs, "morning Ken, hey did you see the play-offs last night...?"

There is no time for bonding,
believe me,
no time

Our European Days

Your histories slid that final day
across fading fragments of mine,
our empires sketched their
piled-up fallen,
and the forensic trace of frost, of light,
little good to students gathered on their knees
prodding our smoking aftermath;

your history
fell around me - today,
like wood-carved windows
meet Maltese
streets -
and childless couples who unfold curtains - but nothing more;

When they fumbled finger after finger through that rubble,
what could they see?
a local-vineyard glass emptied of you, perhaps topped up for me?

Sligo Landscape, January

By glut of bulbous stone
sunk in haggard land,

by ceaseless march of fist
in stiffened militia wall -

these stoic regiments
mark and rank where time begins;

Their discs are blistered on clockwork disc,
their backbone entwined in flesh, their hands tense as corpse in icy-soil -

and the daring conclaves of thistle
are drizzle-pierced mast hoarding virgin's stone.

A caustic sea
washes remnants, kernels, on Ben Bulben's

withered shaft -
there is a living-spirit within,

a sandwort-healed aeon -
raised-up for bidding;

Up from the thaws of moistened soil
fingertips untangled -

handprint
framing mordant sea, the arriving fold of crystal-whitened beach

Maritime

1.
In Youghal
half-buried railway lies
tanned in slivered-browns,
muck and fauna
fend off sea;

2.
The thrill sharpens the solo cut of strand -
in *Perks' Arcade*
a scream of kids
shadow muck and bending rust,
sailors' solar-eyed moonlight probes.

3.
Maritime is my favourite noun,
grappling the music of rumbling rope;
the women-folk
rhyming notions
of summer rains,
and chants of mead-moistened dusk.

4.
It's easy to tell a man who earned his beard,
faces dangling in thickened bush -
men who'll wrestle bears
when ship reaches Canadian shores,
arms knotted with mountain terrain.
Maritime hands cracking the furrows - of departed oak.

5.
Rory Gallagher's *Maritime* collects glasses from clinks of drizzled night,
Youghal sinking below the butter-cupped sun;
the grease-incense lingers - from bruised bumper-car battalions,
from the song-less amusement arcade.
I think of trains no longer leaving here,
the smell of fish heading in crates homewards to Cork,
my father and me sat here in 1981 -
a pleasant gent in a pinstripe-suit
mistook his *Maritime* shadow for the *Perks' Amusement Arcade* boss

The Scene Where the Weeds are Plucked in *Lamb*; 1985

The muck barely hides its sinews,
something stirring, half-nude, half-shamed, the commune of hands
with stories and dogma
that squelch in rusted-river,
on cursed frosty soil.

Everything's stained with dripping ink
from Max Weber's ironic pen -
and irony stings like Heaven's fire
on boy's jangling-aching rib -,
nails bulged with muck like the scholar's pen in doubt -
in this sour and scorched shallow earth.

The smell of the old bastard's braised leather
will bring lives back
to our subterranean skin; by hook or by crook it somehow will

Highway of the Resurrections
(For Terry Kath and Officer John Wintergreen)

For the dust and sand
I say - rise brothers/sisters, rise,
for the water that trickles down from scalded stone,
I say - rise lovers, rise,
for the Volkswagen camper vans in my dreams
I say, I will arise, I will be born again,
and for you, enthroned on road, un-stringed marionette,
for you, a face hanging everywhere but your skull;

I wish you would rise brother,
I pray you would arise

There Was a Woman Called Mrs. Mooney Who Used to Live a Few Doors Away

I remember nothing of her face;
her name is as close to flesh
time will let me re-create;

where she lived
the walls were crumbling,
and the stones spat and hissed on damp-lime ground -

as if confused with
stiletto-sharpened cliff
bare-chested

gangling French-men climbed -
in a picture-house interlude film,
from 1982.

When we last called on Mrs. Mooney
there was a parcel flumped behind her door,
it filled up her sepia-clothing, and the stamp was the physiog-
nomy of her closing stare,

when the blue-lights had gone
and her front-door coughed shut -
some plaster keenly fell,

and a French-man back on earth
wept for his lost *chérie*,
the walls of dust settling on barren rocky soil

You Remind Me Of Sir Nigel Gresley's Mallard

From time to time
electricity gave your flesh some semblance of self,
something poured music through your blood,
something flashed like summer-fires in forests
across the stardust that shimmered on your silent lips;
and that something would then unplug itself from you;
and your left fist
and your right fist
moved
like the wheels of *The Mallard*
on July the 3rd, 1938,
and the speed you reached
was comparable with the time it took
to reach the nearest available loo,
and put your fingers down your throat
and forgive yourself
before I had the chance,
and I would think of *The Mallard,*
before speech had set out to join us,
and you were hoovering and cleaning at 5am with eyes like Keith Moon,
and the kind of fire in your blood that kills payless grafters -
in shithole factories in piss-poor countries;
and I would admire *The Mallard*'s beautiful royal-blue body,
its streamlined shape,
its hiss of steam and throbbing chug,
and how far it could push
without thinking,
and for all its beauty
how fascist it looked,
with 1939 only a few months away

Spain

Like Laurie Lee's soles
invited
cursed radiated stone,
earth crept its chasms inward -
warming bones in Spanish flesh,
warning him too - of little doubt;

A contrast was that vision -
his dust-caved nose
in libraries of troubadour song,
the touch of hand
scorched red, now a creeping blue,
the overhanging mysteries

and their wind-howled dance - through the grief
and needless silence - of a single sanguine tree.
From rib-cage to dust-picked neck
and alone to Segovia's song, its breast-plated rock
where feet cut death's sundried shadows free,
on scorched and chalky earth,
writing scripts for the tombs of sinking land.

The smokey bone of
skeleton
is piled upon pile, the
dust hovering; it's starting to itch...

Moon

Moon, bide your time;
you 1950s street-corner spiv,
you turn our bodies back
before your sister earth lets us sink below;
moon, bide your time,
our movements intricate,
the mathematics of love,
the science from which your flesh
gives our random movements shape;
how you smash your lover's light
on the tree's shattered bark,
how you disrupt the logic
on the snail's streaks of weeping moss,
oh, moon, are you raging now?
as we suss your coin-spinner's con,
our shapes growing, our movements multiply,
moonlight - come find us,
you gum chewing street-corner spiv

The Farrier
(For Mother and Father)

Sparks, a sheen of
brown shines back
evening's glare,
his smooth-tanned leather pouch -
a legion of blistered secrets -
how horseshoes find that Grecian curve,
the rasping clink heavy on its anvil brethren;
then tea-time cools the humid girth, of panting brick,
in bend of back, regimental still.
Sparks resume,
reaching into hell, corporal's mustache, the thirst of
smoke on helpless linen *"say nothing to your mother"*
a nervous smile, scalp hushed on the rickets of half-arsed roof,
cowboy builders' job, Summer 1975;
the kitchen rumbles, a feminine purr,
vox aeterna,
turf-mounds stuff the yard's whitewashed-belly, Winter 1979

McKenna's *Bóthairín,* Summer 1984
(For Michelle Goddard)

1.
Thickets sense Nemain's breeze, then willingly ripple,
slim as schoolboys clad
in blood-depth slacks;
A farmer's fingers turn robin-red, sensing
high noon's slow windless-arch.

2.
When affordable housing rumbles down McKenna's *Bóthairín,*
the price of thickets ripped from soil
will measure a plotted brick to every thrushes' nest -
on every digger's claw a blood-clot laneway ends its day,
an erased summer's empire - sketched starless on thickened
bulging black.

3.
And these thickets I watch bleeding
while my parents butter icy-lotions on angered skin,
are blacker than the soot-caked paint of Mick Jagger's sorrow,
darker than the sky-choked night
of unloved prancing wheat

People Don't Just Stop Drinking

Let's hear what booze has to say,
how tired it got of
2 week old babies, nested in a
cradle of responsible living,
its fear of 68 year old men
whose lives were clawed in long uninterrupted streaks
of tobacco-stained fingernails down a boulevard of termite
eaten bars.
Let's hear what booze has to say, why it had to leave its
clientele behind,
switching brands to exciting young men who
speak in wildfires of *lols*, and duck-faced ceremonies
gathered at the ellipsis of the camera's frigid edge,
who look for women who say four letter words they object to
when sober,
when they describe sisters' husbands who spend too long
in the office,
leaving their jackets on the back of chairs with ties un-knotted,
in Lebanese restaurants;
it's true, people don't stop drinking, booze grows tired of them;

How about us - 14 weeks free from our habitat,
"on the dry" the common parlance;
let's crack this bottle open, just one more time,
hear if it's true, what the booze has to say,

ties loosened a little...

Italia, Ottobre
(For John Greene and Enda Carr)

What remains of sundown
makes its own way west,

and the crimson-fragments
follow,

swirling round firs like Pompeii mist -
the broken surf of pensioned leaves

like plotted-coups of ancient Rome.
The farmers' fingers argued on and on 'til dusk,

an abacus of un-ripened seed;
and the curtained crimson mourns their deceit -

in bloodied-fist on
reddened-brick,

the witnessing olives'
effigy, for the rumble and crunch of Fiat rubber.

And the day made its own way west,
the crimson fragments catching up,

a volley of geese ripped from narrowed path,
mother's head tilted to an easing trot…

Tuone Udaina

And rocks commence their bustled crumble,
grey-steel thunder pre-deceases
a curtain-call of speech,
the waters below - breathless, chilly,
mercurial;

But it's dust that clasps your throat,
hunts your penultimate expression
under a paper-flat musing of flesh, paper fluttered
minus pen, blackened-ink oozing for sea;
land and thought are biting descent of childless love, a solo finale.

The tumbling rocks softened your days so precisely, Tuone,
your archaic alphabets dried, scorching your limpid tongue,
motionless, pollen-free;
no earth, no land can warm its spores, your speech you see
lighter than broken Autumn leaves -
a brusque litany of snow falling, on the 10th of June -
each flake melts on the tip of your silenced tone; calendar flattened -
under speechless stone

Australian Postage Stamp 1972 - *Overland Telegraph Line*
(Painted By John Copeland)

The rattling tin-shacks
of moonlight's Morse code
on lines from Darwin to Perth
Newcastle to Geelong,
the *Corroborees* telegraphed in dream-time,
the gangling alpha-male -
body in
gold, black, red,
viscerous talk on glimmering wires

Australian Postage Stamp 1970 - Celebrating National Development
(Painted by Robert Ingpen)

Bauxite's alchemists conjure their aluminium;
soon heads are nodding,
the alchemists
in hard hats and long white coats
(their lives soon slipping on the shine of brand-new clipboards)
phone-up stiff-jawed un-sideburned
men called Clive back in Perth;
Clive's wife's busy writing letters,
bauxite to aluminium
the computer age can't be far behind,
and still not a word back from
that doctor,
no magic there, 9 months that alchemy takes,
not 9 years

She Swore She Would Ride a Scooter Through the Basque Country One Day
(Inspired by the cover art of Karl Geary's Montpelier Parade)

I unraveled every rigid stitch of you,
'til I met your body-sunken legs -
they stood like wobbling stalks,
Feronia-tinted chestnuts - on Karl Geary's *Montpelier Parade.*

As grey as un-painted morgues in France,
greener than your fading eyes,
when simmering pigments howled through engine-room fires;
our nightmare resumed on soggy, but mostly dry land.

You danced around fishing nets
where the harbour nibbled chalky shore,
I followed you -
in the pork-draped windows of Elgoibar,

piazzas
where F. Scott Fitzgerald's shoes
splashed buttermilk promise
on your sienna-seeping brogues.

The Fall crumbled like earthquakes,
under New England espadrilles,
but somehow, I had not changed -
and all that they left of you was ash, waiting for the rain on *Montpelier Parade*

and the knots you swore you'd unwind on Basque Country roads,
are pedals on nearly-rusted bikes,
their soles less-corroded -
than your sand and eyeless-face

Hangover

Blessed Jesus forgive me for I knew exactly what I did,
I'll hide out in Connecticut for a while, change my name to *Smith*

Albino Luciani

You feel the softness of August fruit,
peaches aligned to a tint of human skin,
and softness within,
like a day you traced the height of grass
on your fingertips
before your knees lost sight of your feet,
and the fruits, water-coloured green
RAI TV record on hazy clouds of film;
camera-men quickly trundle back to vans,
their footsteps soon behind you,
your bible eased
on the soothe of grass,
the taste of peach on prayer-softened
tongue -
as pink as the Tuscan skies,
when prayers left the mouth
before they reached the soul

When The Sligo Liner Passes Through Maynooth Again

For John Sullivan (Station Master, Maynooth, County Kildare, 1980s)

"He hangs in shades the orange bright..."
Andrew Marvell

Evenings came,
evergreens inviting piquant egress,
thickened dog barks
drenched and wrung - in parapets of rain;

the fields round here
watched our moon-fat faces
flee schoolyard tannoy
for the brace of sizzling sun,

and in evening's plunge
we kissed our knees on wheat-whispered stalks,
Bell Liners
clicking, jangling past -

and in the clickety-clack of hazy summers
diesel guts turned nights to a flaxen cameo of brown -
a *141*'s roaring belly
chewed sundown - onwards through Kilcock

Seasons

Winter
Baldur's in heat;
we hear him scheme through crow-clutched trees,
his peninsula's gurgle
as snow-gloss brook counts swollen fold,
one upon the other,
his blackened wings almost bare -
and those who hear this,
murmur their replies -
darkness taking sudden flight; in enveloping Winter.

Spring
Spread across the soil
the painter's touch is soft,
tempted immortals raise their glass.
The chills are staggered - somewhat,
but the icy-tone has mellowed
to a colour lite-blue on powdered breath.
Equal to slushy sod
are yellows, greens, the fleeting flash of finch -
roofless, baptised - for newly spawned Spring.

Summer
The river-bank seems dense;
perhaps under-grown,
ripe for each jangling-shelved country farm;
these are the seasons we end-up bombarded
with well meaning home-made soap,
from neighbours, from women who carry eggs
in marsupial aprons;
July takes these twisted plasmic veins

in Kaleidoscope forms of dusk -
in music where jam-jars croon along;
in Summer.

Autumn
Though the fires are quenched,
colours stay bone-dry on every touch,
bruised-red, the bullied beast of brown -
and the naked bones of trees re-dressed;
soon will come the greys,
billowing like smoke from farmland pyres -
pirouette leaves marching
to an old-time harvest waltz.
We watched Stephen Foster gather twigs outside,
pencil clutched like infant, in the grooves of sun-pinkened ear,
his dust-brushed coat
made from the sparks of cindered Autumn

Outposts
For Balasi Salvador

"*Asko daki zaharrak, erakutsi beharrak*"
Old Basque Proverb

A soon-strayed cat
caresses coal-dust car-park corners;
rain arrives.
It makes itself known, this kith of fog -

a low-hung conifer takes its bait.
I looked for harbours
where shores mounted
benevolent grey, stones simply did what gods

thundered,
puke-green whips of scattered weed -
Finistère, Biscay,
ports of scraggy feline mounds filling Neptune's reckless hope -

outside of un-clocked hours - and idle dismembered days.
I watch strayed shapes
cut their sails through sudden greys; walls pressed on seas
of unwatered dim -

I feel at ease with Wednesdays, their harbours and fogs,
their feline strays paw-printed in soot

The Crucifixion of Jeffrey Hunter, 1969

I watched him - a sanguine touch of Christ,
when tonight's sky played its last audition;
Aramaic bled in Technicolor pink,
indexed in its coercive cirrus scribes.

His
bone-rust nacreous
is censored by whip-cracked wrists,
a cross clattering on staircase -

the claret evening descent;
crown of thorns -
throbbing crimson skull,
and dusk has announced its schedule for tonight -

ladies and gentlemen
if you could please remain patient;
our show will unfold
to shroud his ascent - skull-flat wines turned messianic-red

An Cois Farraige, Gaoth Dobhair

I mo bhéal, bhí an ghaoth
ag caint,

agus ar an talamh
bhí an gaineamh ag éisteacht,

agus na beirt
ag damsha sa spéir,

agus misé, gan focail,
agus an domhain, ina n-aonar;

an gaineamh agus an ghaoth - ag damhsa,
ag gáire, ag magadh...

Goddess

Mortal, immortal,
fingers begging sun,

sun loving man,
as wife, as womb, as one

Evening

Reason, I sacrifice you to the evening breeze.
Aime Cesaire

Perched on evening's oars
cautions oscillate;
a moment tracing brittle day,

an artist rising on electric shore;
by the water's cloud-beaten edge
I've embraced sudden land - humming with light

Side Street Buildings, Irish Seaside Towns

Lilac haunts the fronts,
low-cut roofs
the Moorish decoys
that shyster birds dipping in from sea,

the lanes so thin, the colours touch,
Venice orange, cleric's grey,
and the music the *Smithwicks* bottle sings
explodes in birds in sea-knotted wind

Raymond Carver's Little Black Book of Muses

Remember this: an orphaned baseball mitt is
prime metaphor for drug or alcohol abuse,
drug or booze abuse - is our metaphor for war;

War naturally was declared - in that 1950s *World Series,*
where the greaseballs and a second rate cabaret hack
had so much cabbage in their pockets the following Tuesday

even he could've
gotten in on their act; if he knew who
sat where at mass, if only he went to mass,

and the series of whiskey-waxed sorrows should recline
at glacier's pace to Adderley and Coltrane,
evening by evening above a city so thick in orange

it will start a fire in his 7th cocktail of 10,
leaving *O'Halloran*'s bar on the corner of Jones and Madison,
coughing up the dust his borrowed coat mimics
Donald O'Connor beneath;

and the playful Marciano jabs at an understanding cop
serenade the halitosis grumbled Hail Mary hex,
on insurance salesmen

whose knuckles
make love to his door
every second day -

their wives hoping
to never see

their gawrsh gadzooks Jimmy Stoowart faces once again.

It's the way the ice plunks his glass, he reckons,
is like the way the 8 ball runs from white,
so alone, Bourbon-breath dollars blocking its every plot and escape
-

war, no longer its option, just total surrender.
The thinning shine of skyscrapers
begged Heaven to pack their bones with a little more meat,
his window's

its confession box
voyeurs stare beyond,
to see if his soul is as childless, as his leather-boned mitts - alone,

without a war left to go to,
better chat
with Hemingway, and Frankie Machine -

boys called Chad and Sammy
still wondering, if he will ever hand them back
their tanned and lifeless ball, watching mitts cautious, from the
bowels of the 7th floor

Ploughed Field Near Confey Railway Station, County Kildare

For Heather Stewart

1.
Life nurtures every line,
in every scratch of twig
rubbing sky -

there is sun,
there is moon,
day-fall an urge of cheek on milky bone;

2.
The night shimmers
on lyrics of
sun-ripened mud,

life
a spill of words from gurgling pond -
its tongues stall; gathering speech from translated stars -
trickling, peering...

An Afterthought (Laytown Beach, County Meath)

"...a new life, a new friend, a new love, a new country."
Anaïs Nin

Her wind-lashed script extinguished me,
its antique speech a hiss on whitened surf;
this journey now belongs to me;

my longhand's gruff, ashen through
slivers of time -
though fingertips ordain my stars.

A cadence
of living water
speaks little for that sea, far far behind -

soil squeezed from stone,
feet chiming on shingled beach;
a lighthouse draws me closer, its neoteric script reads like
mine, its wrap-dress ocean-green...

Pski's Porch Publishing was formed July 2012, to make books for people who like people who like books. We hope we have some small successes.
www.pskisporch.com.

323 East Avenue
Lockport, NY 14094
www.pskisporch.com

www.ingramcontent.com/pod-product-compliance
Lightning Source LLC
Chambersburg PA
CBHW060321050426
42449CB00011B/2589